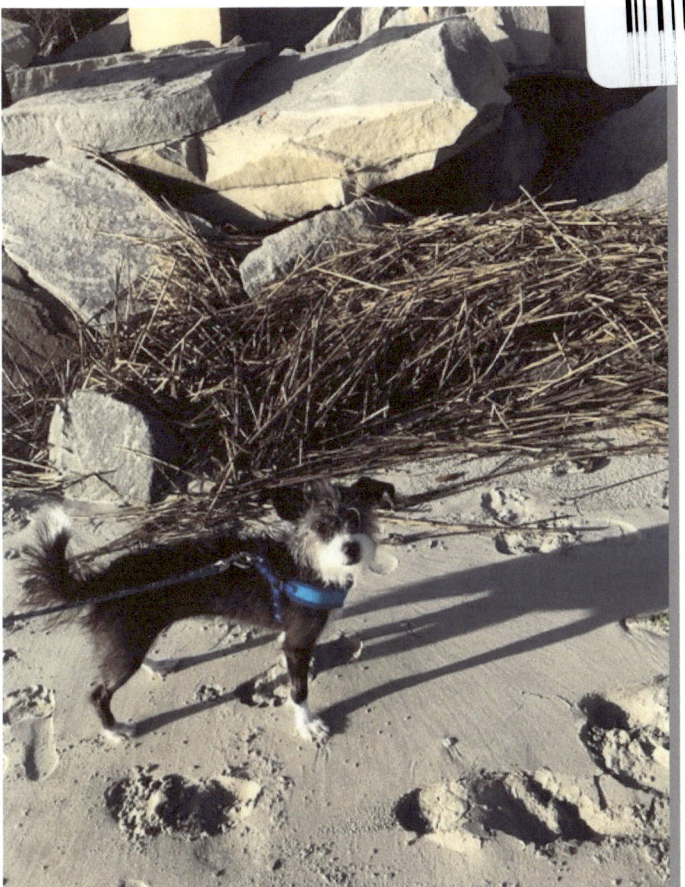

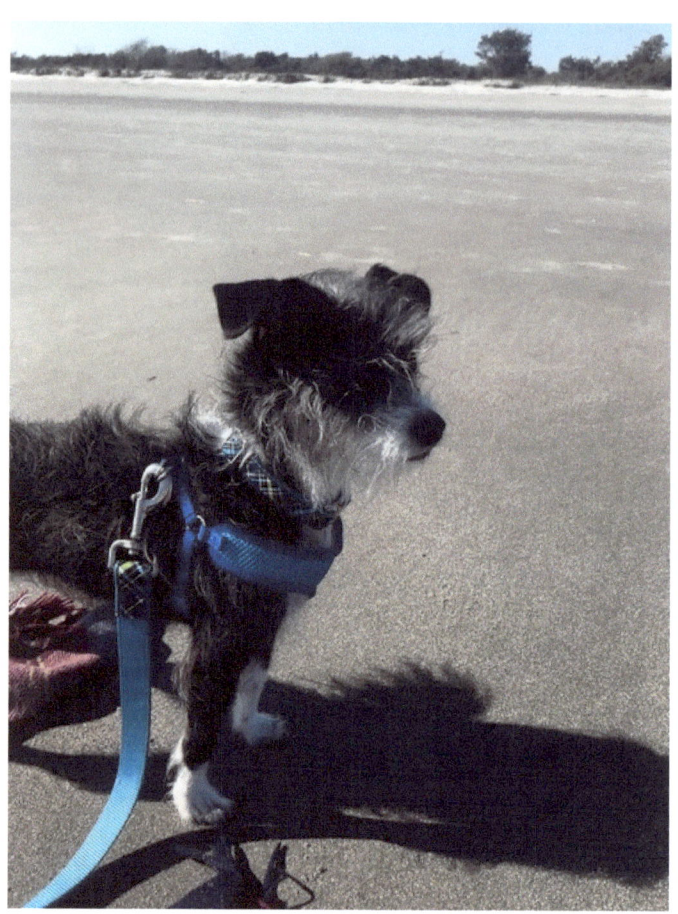

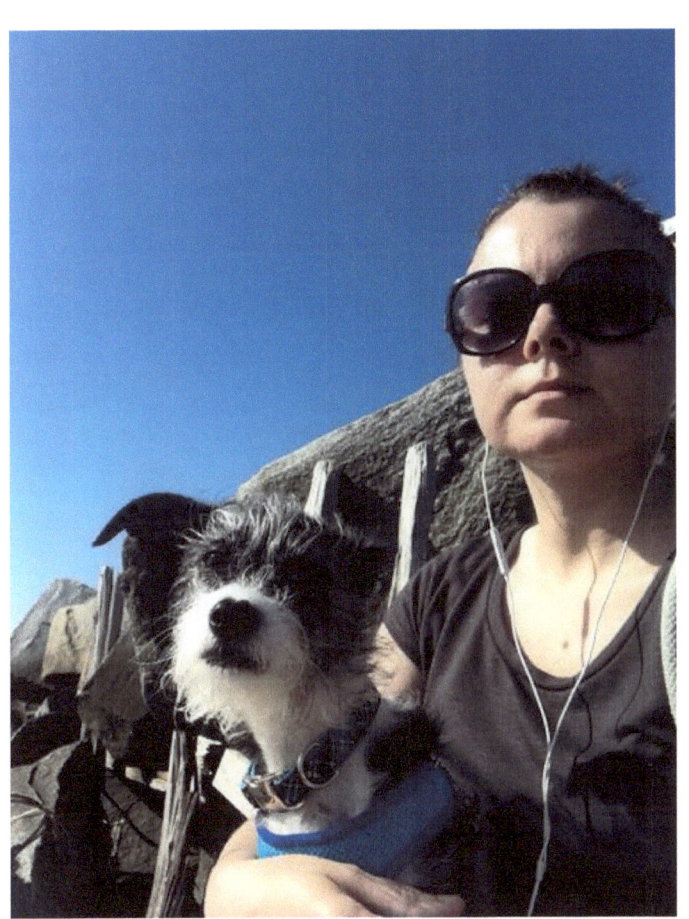

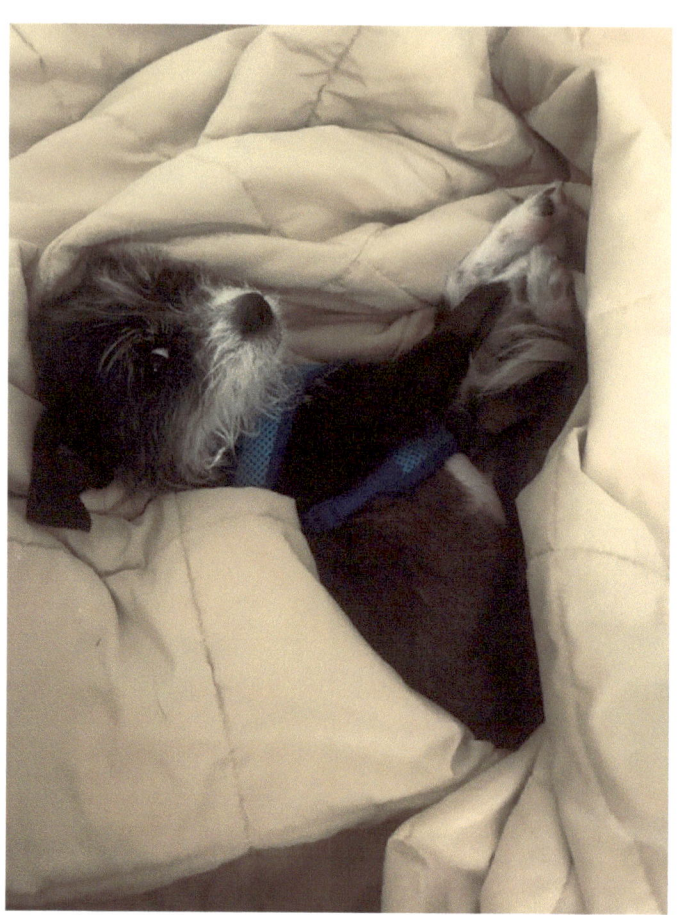

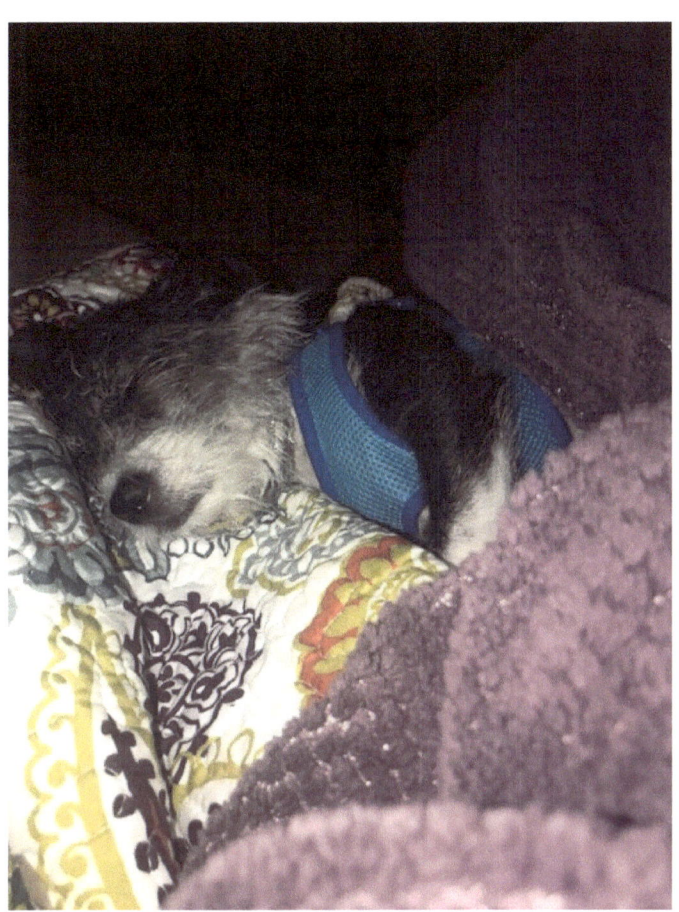

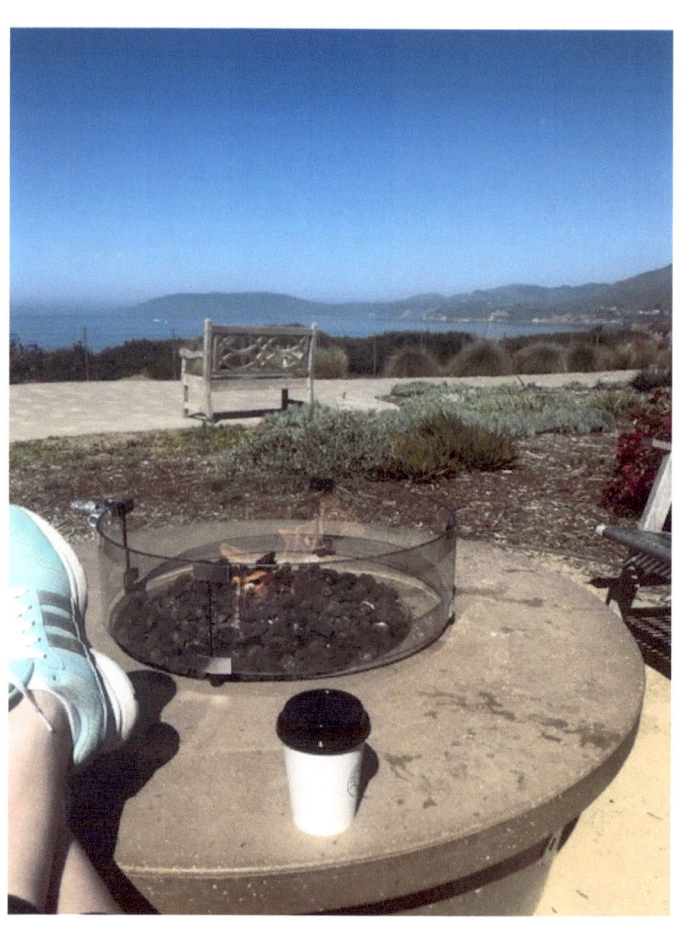

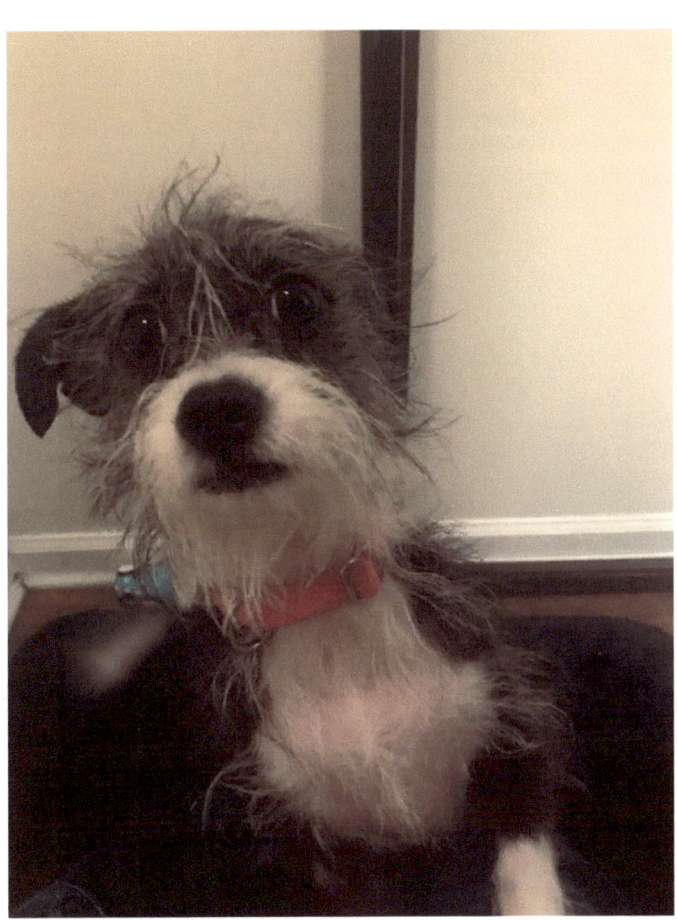

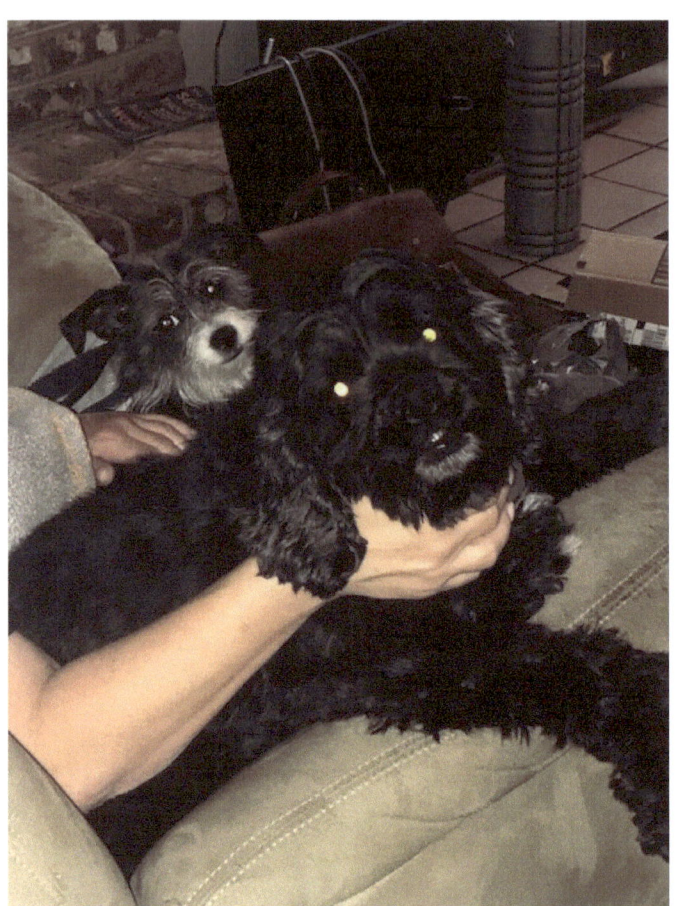

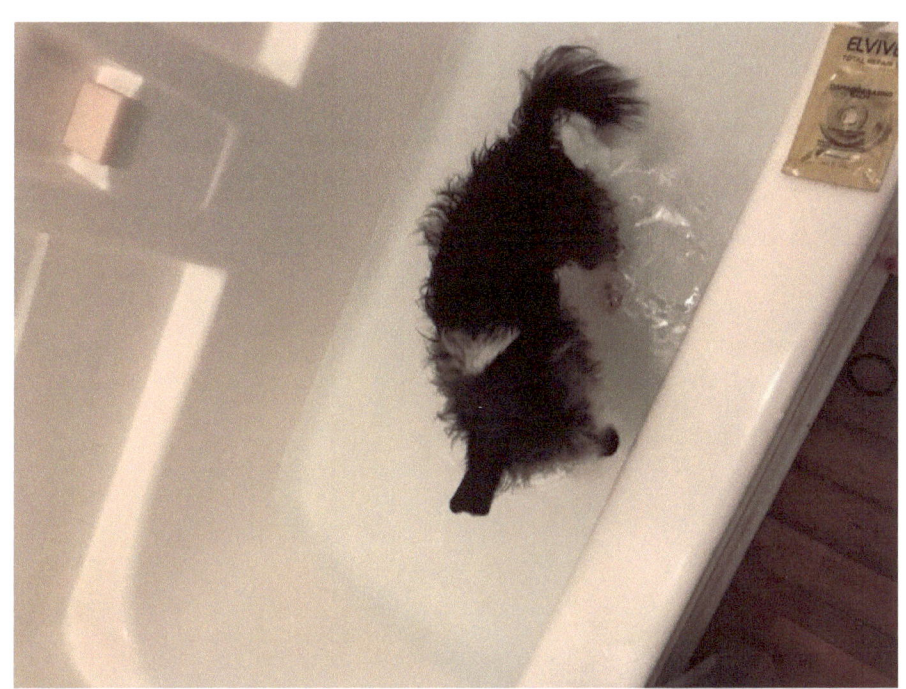

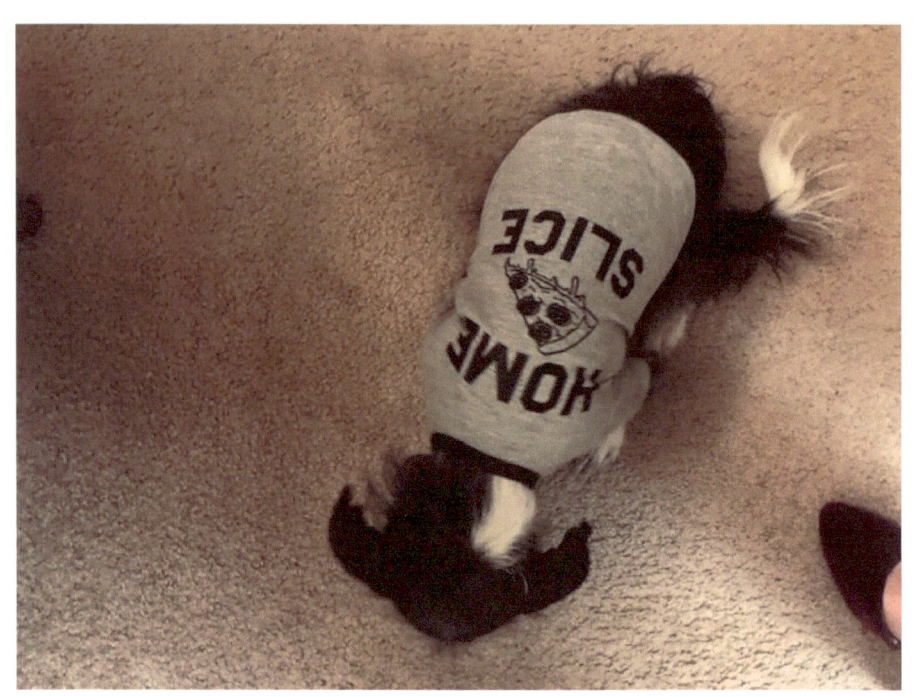

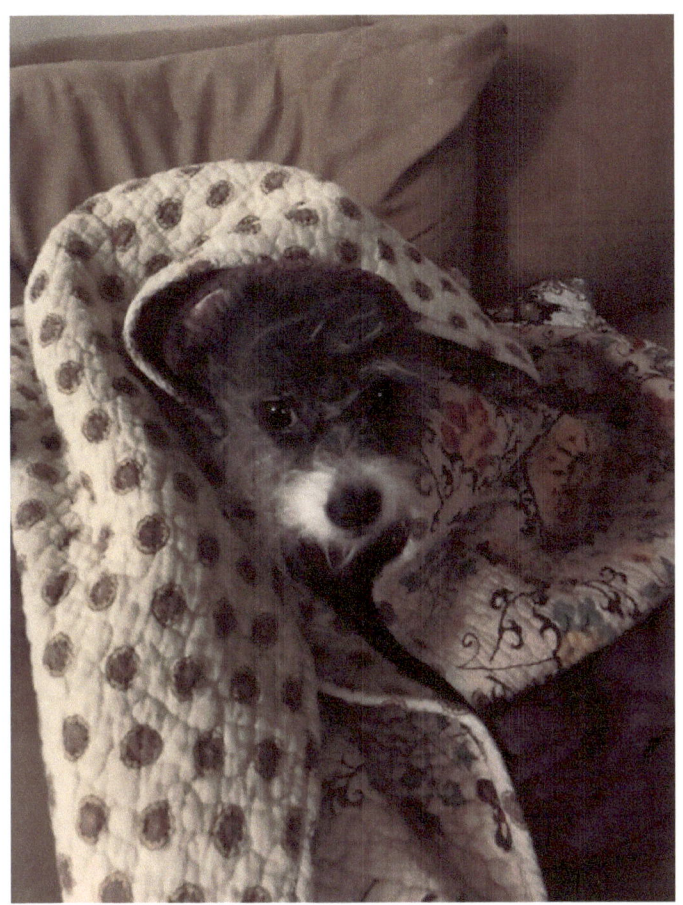

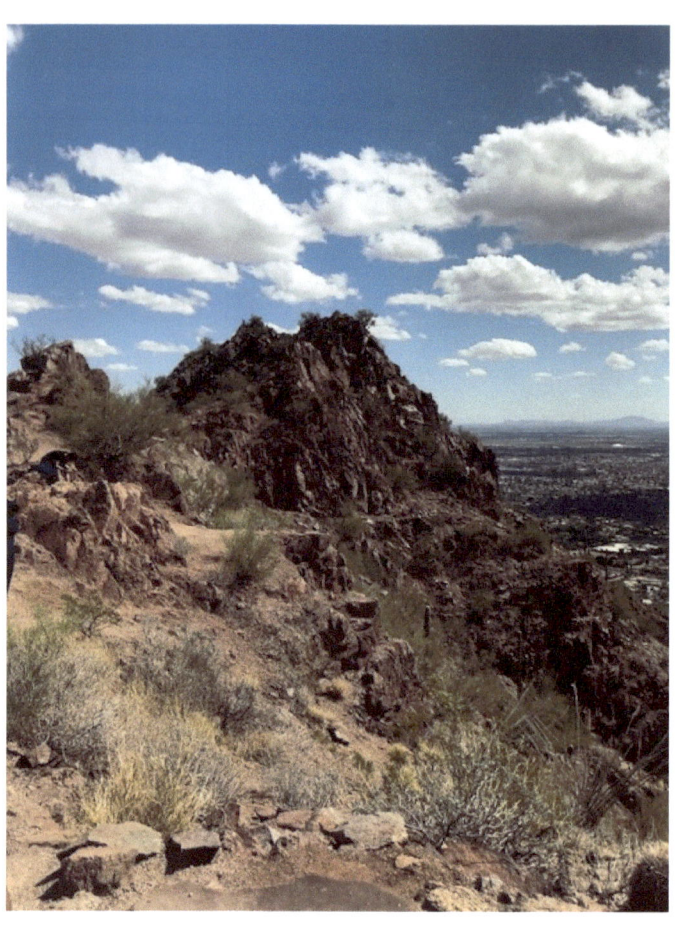

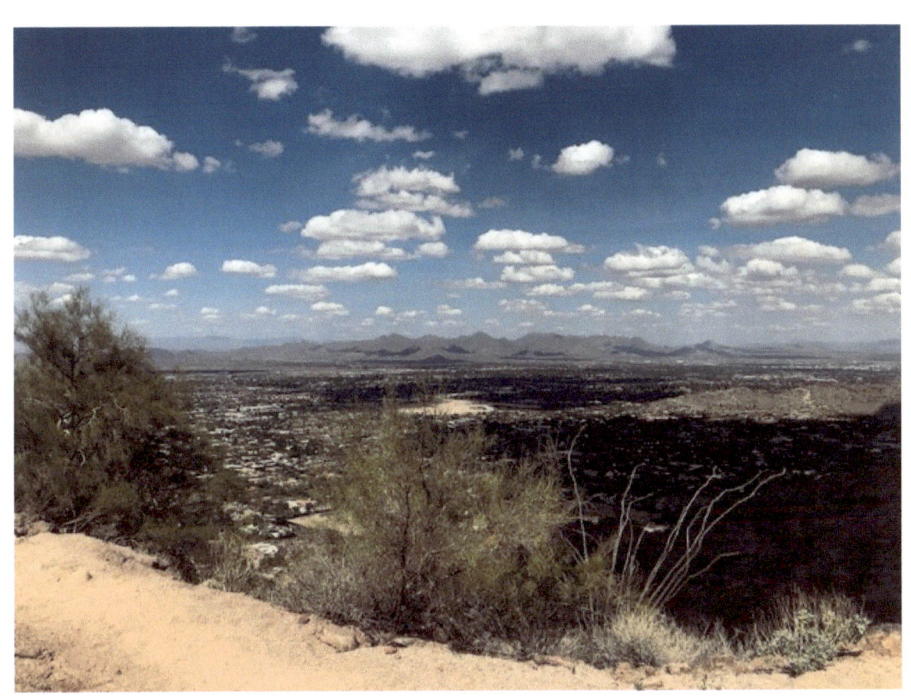

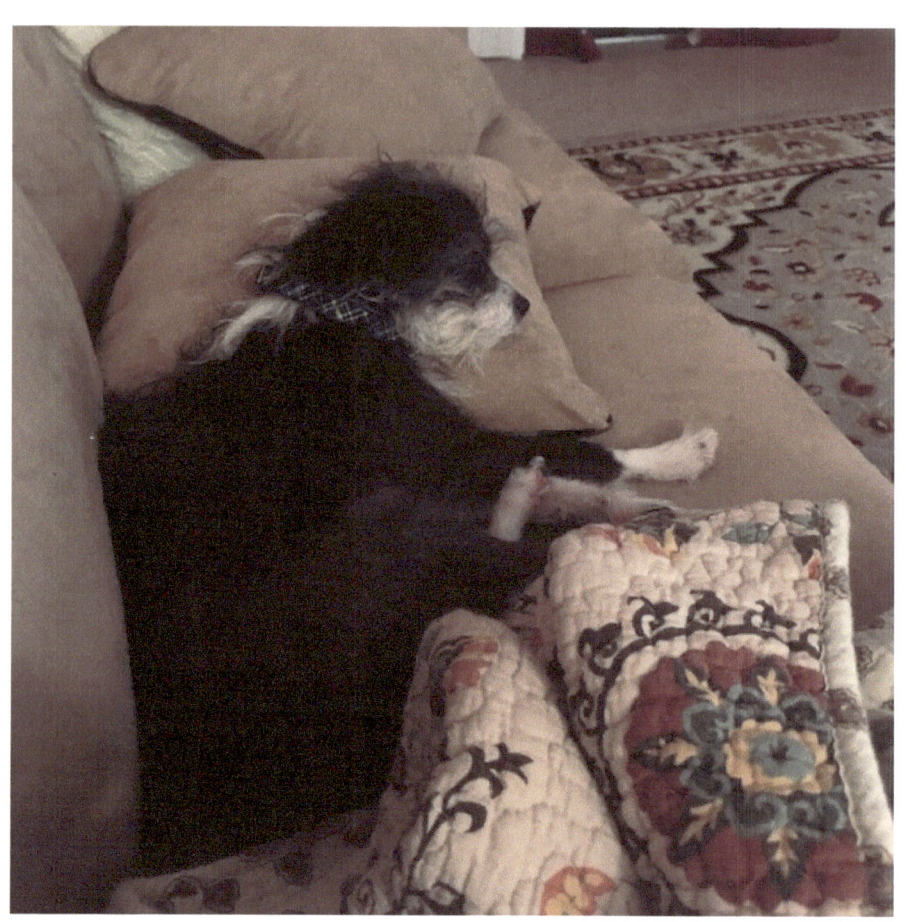

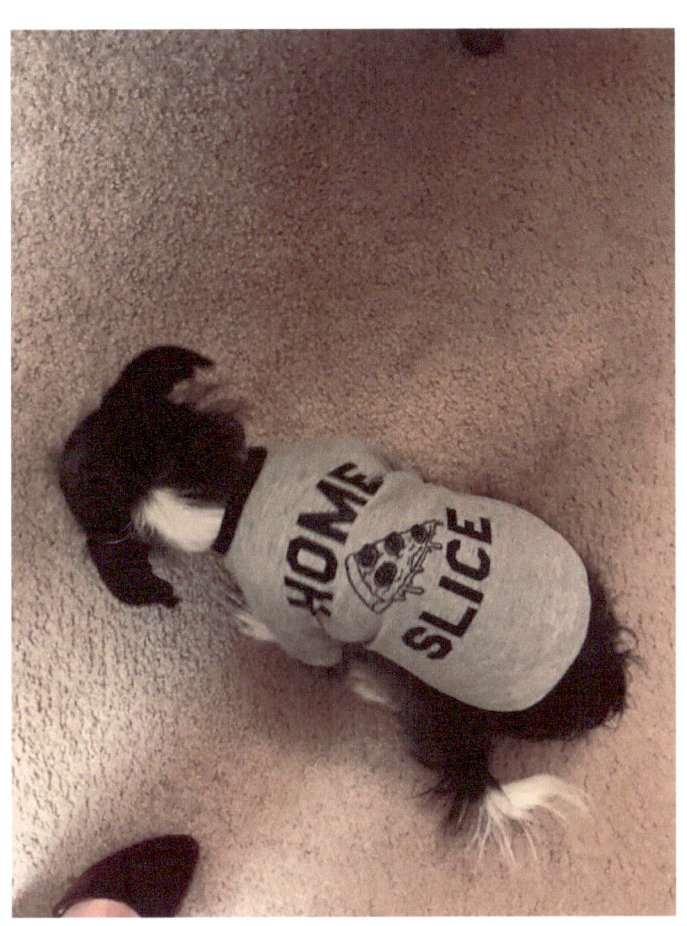

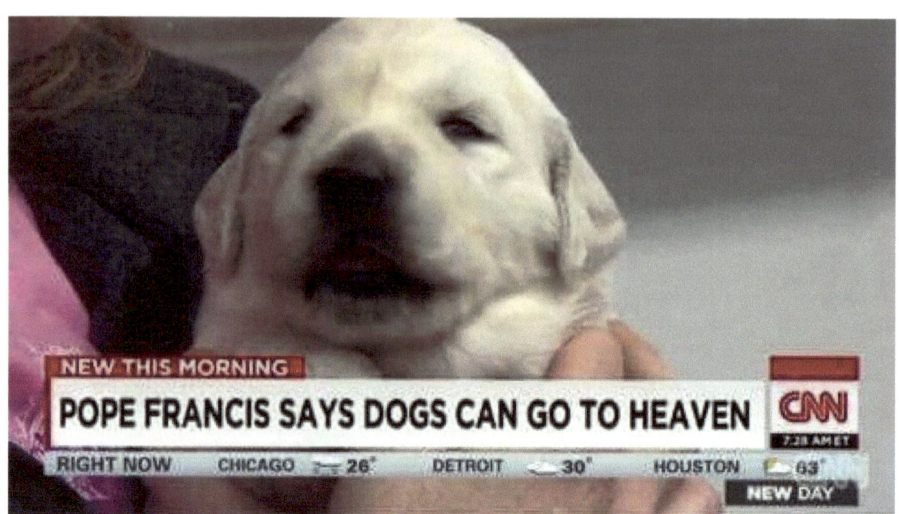

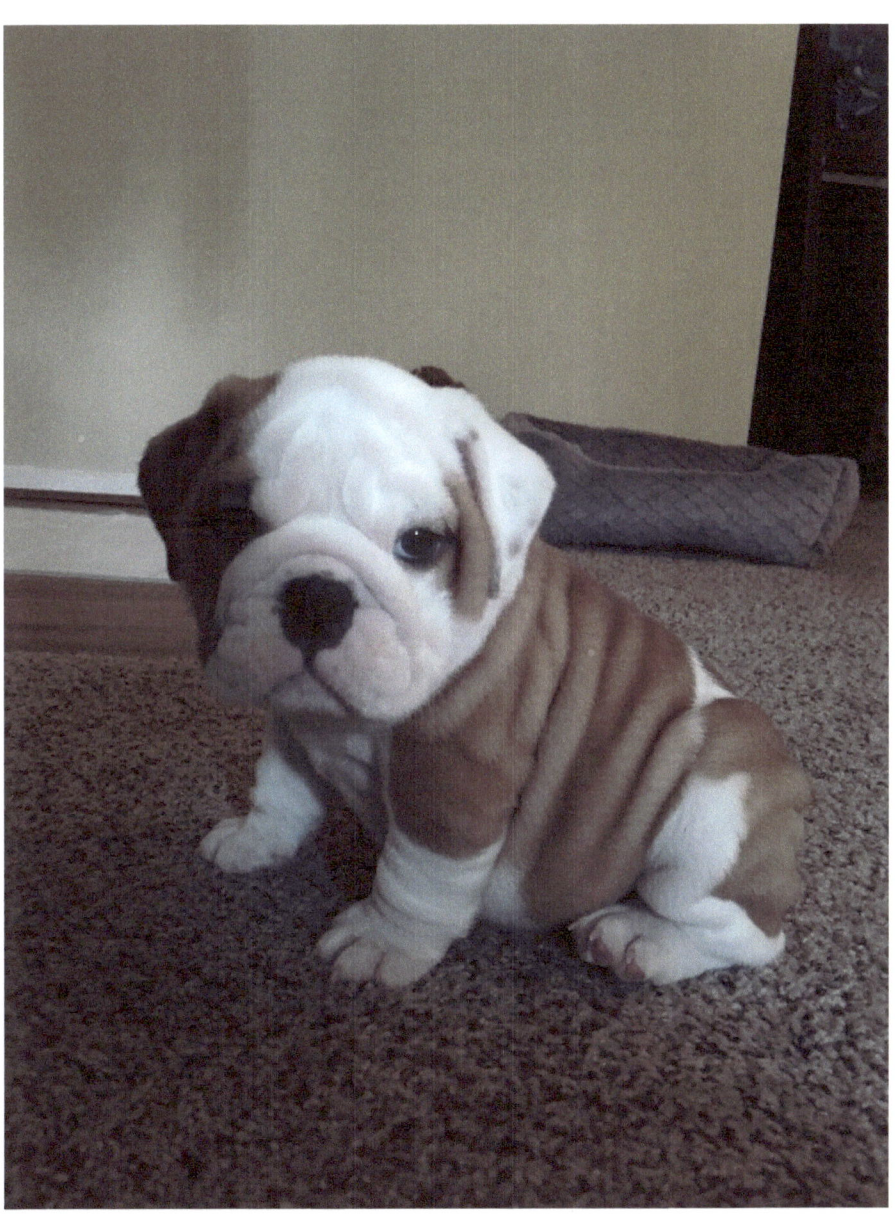

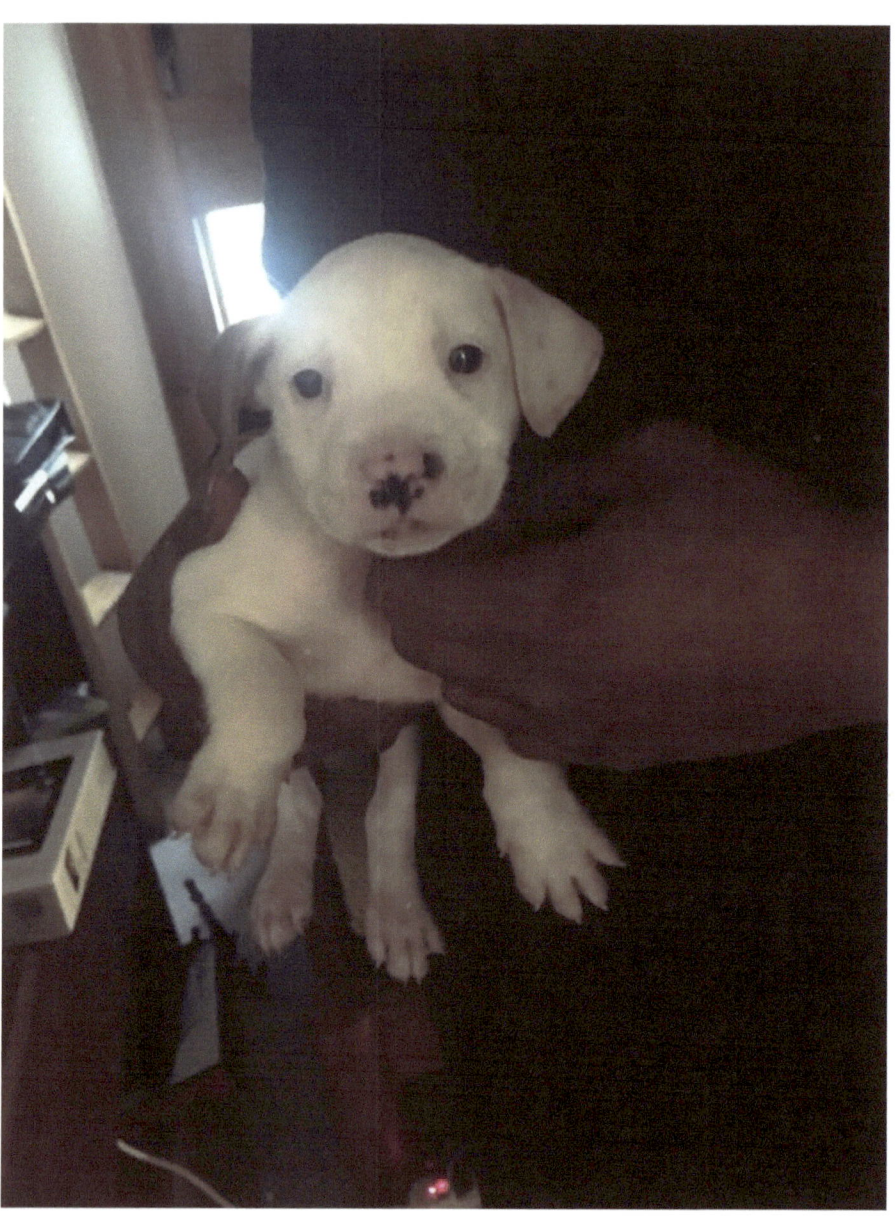

There's no such thing as a perfect nigh-

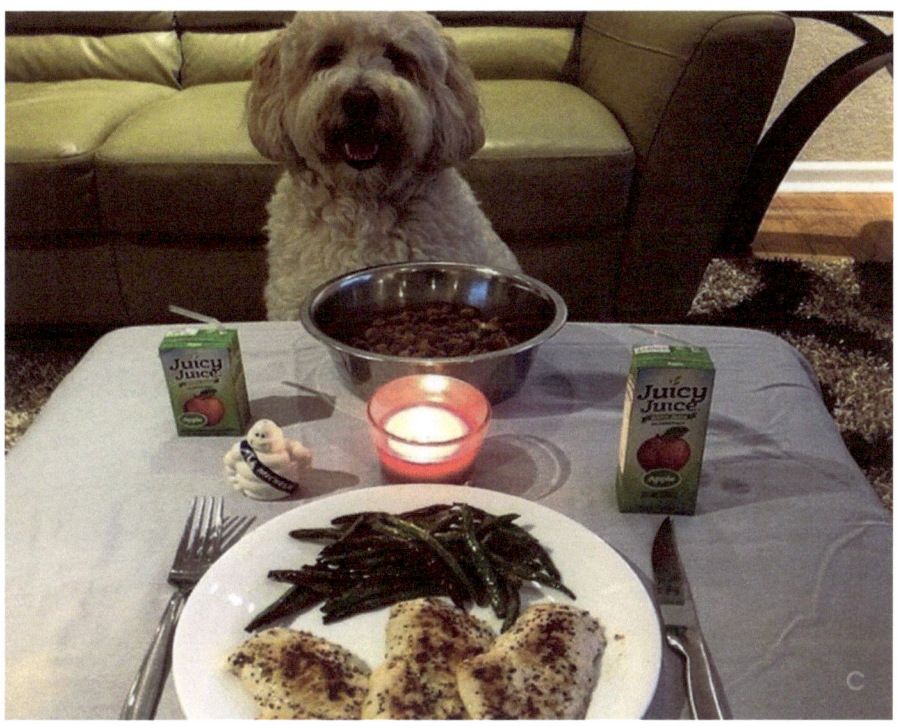

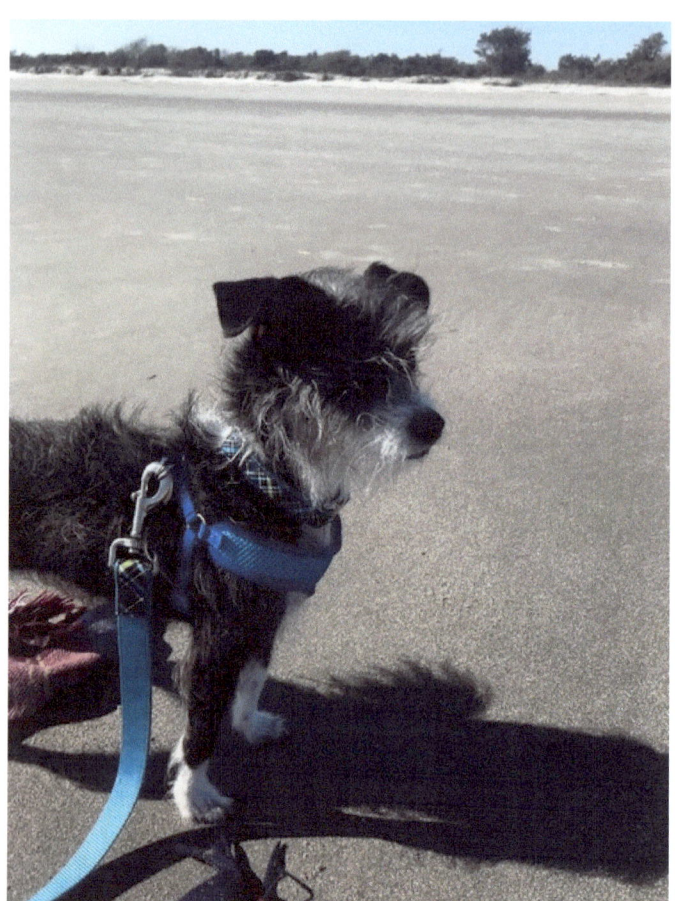

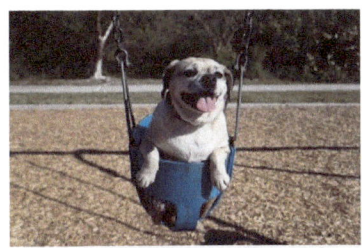

MY PARENTS ARE AT DISNEYLAND AND JUST SENT ME THIS

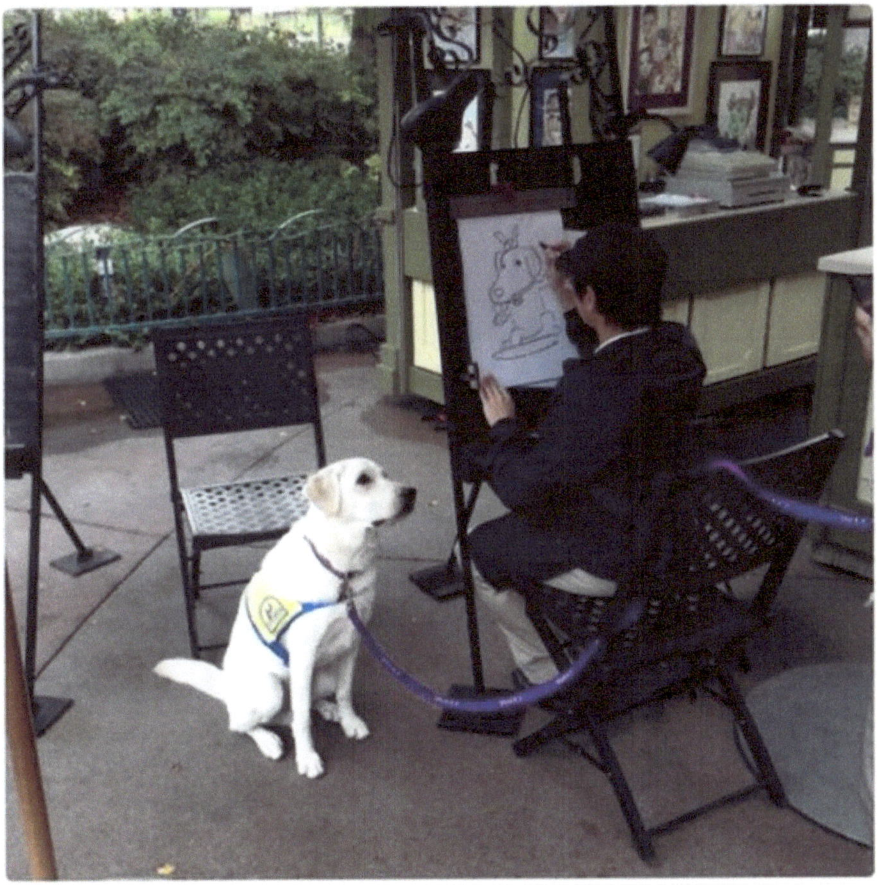

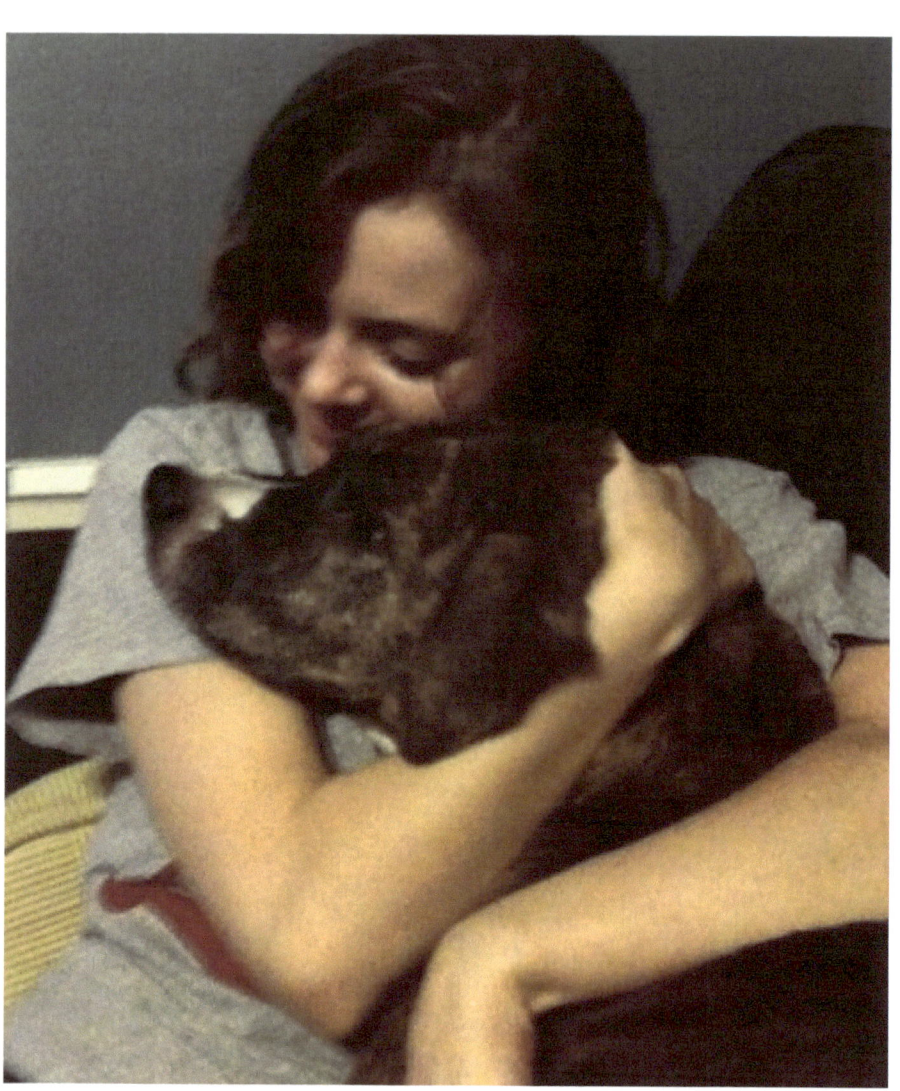

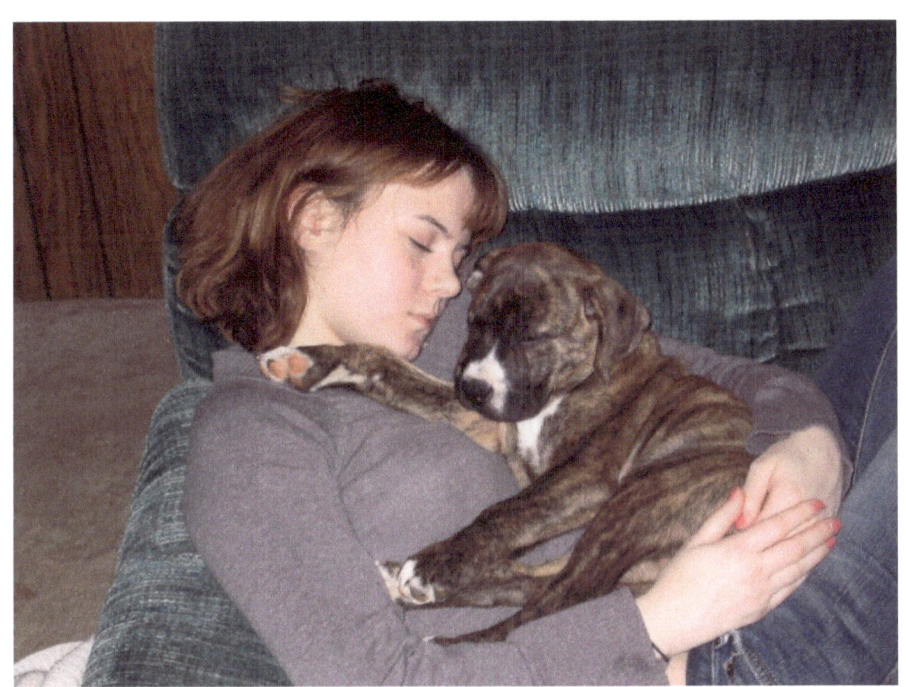

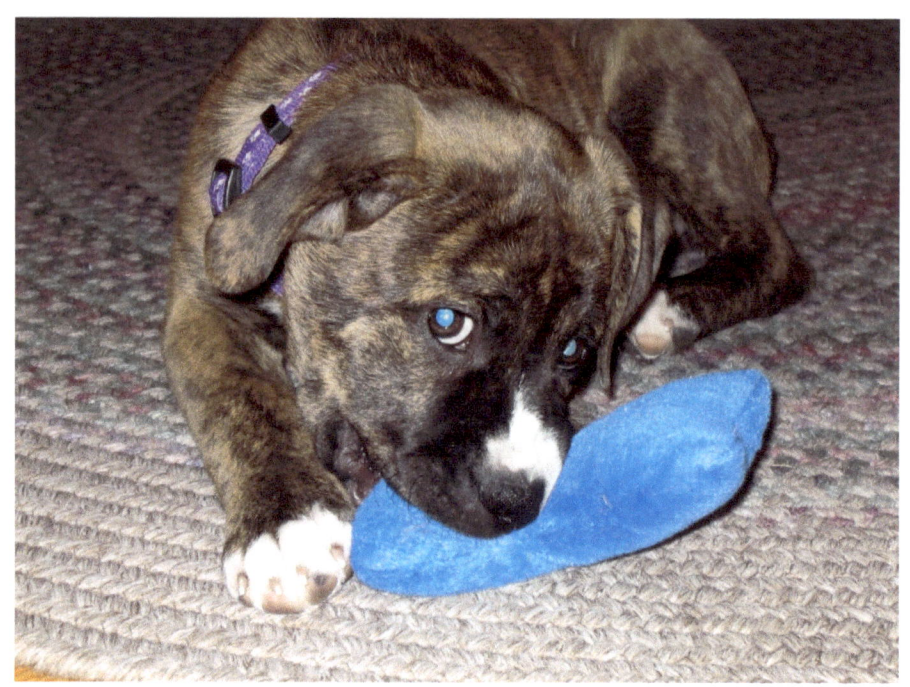

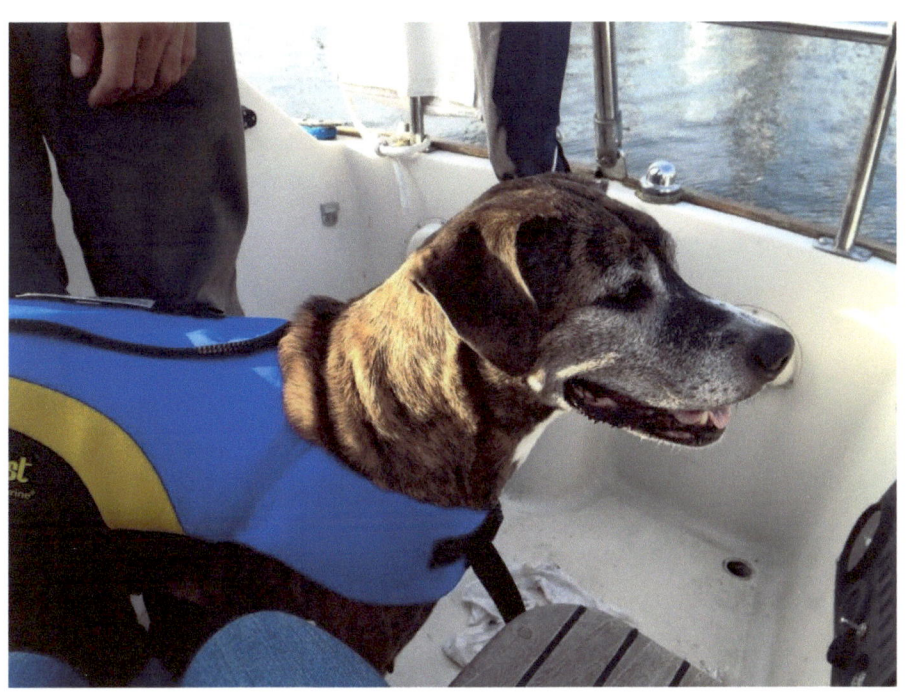

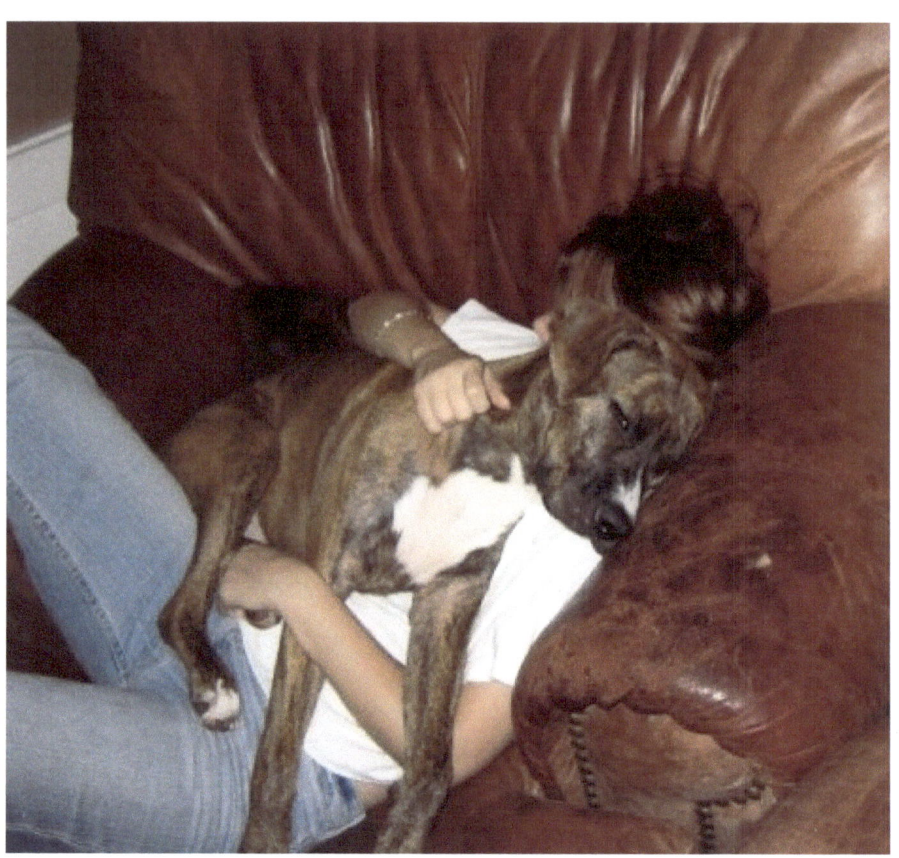

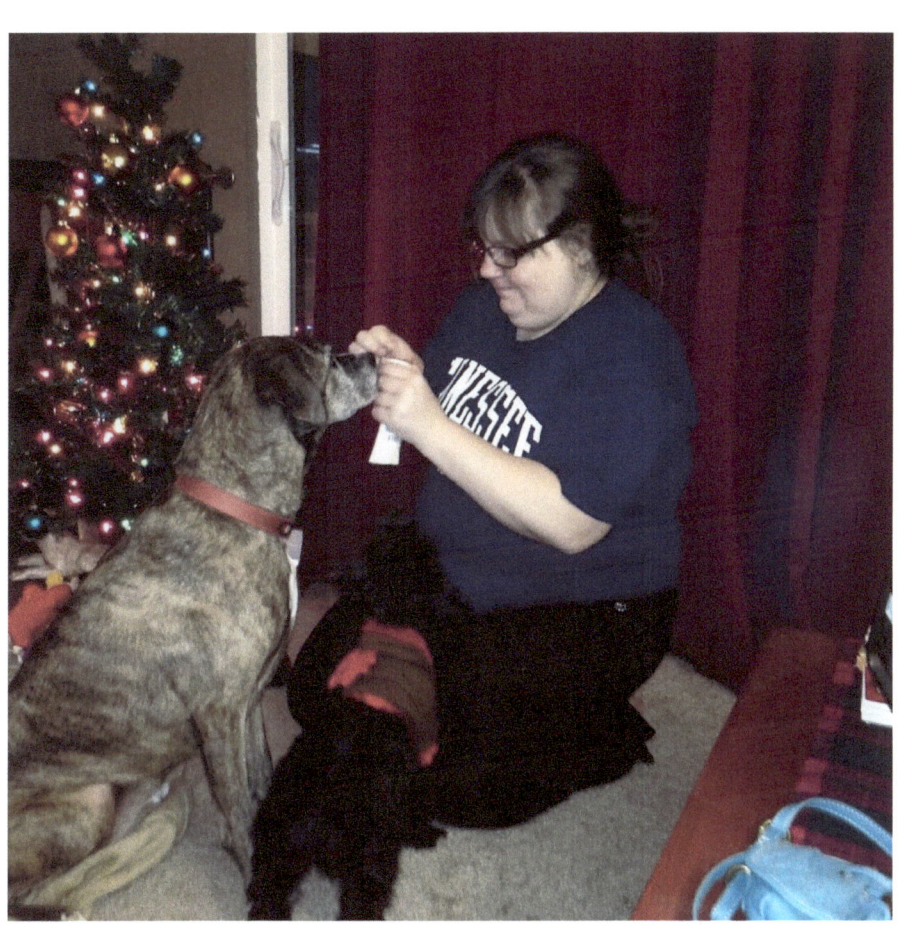

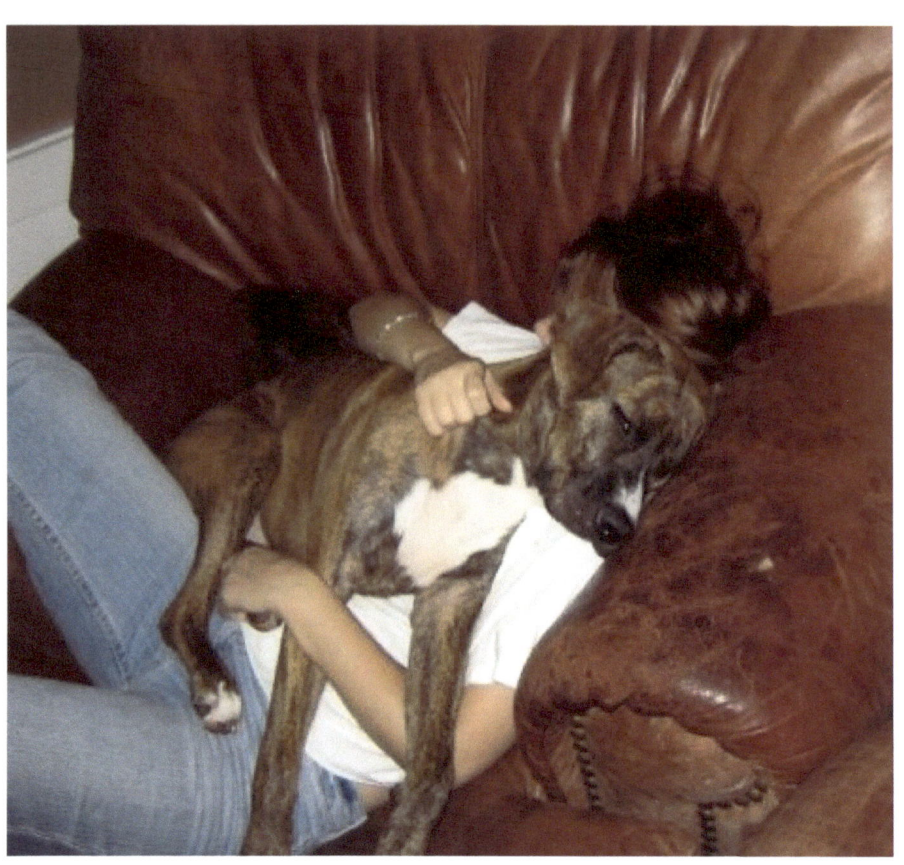

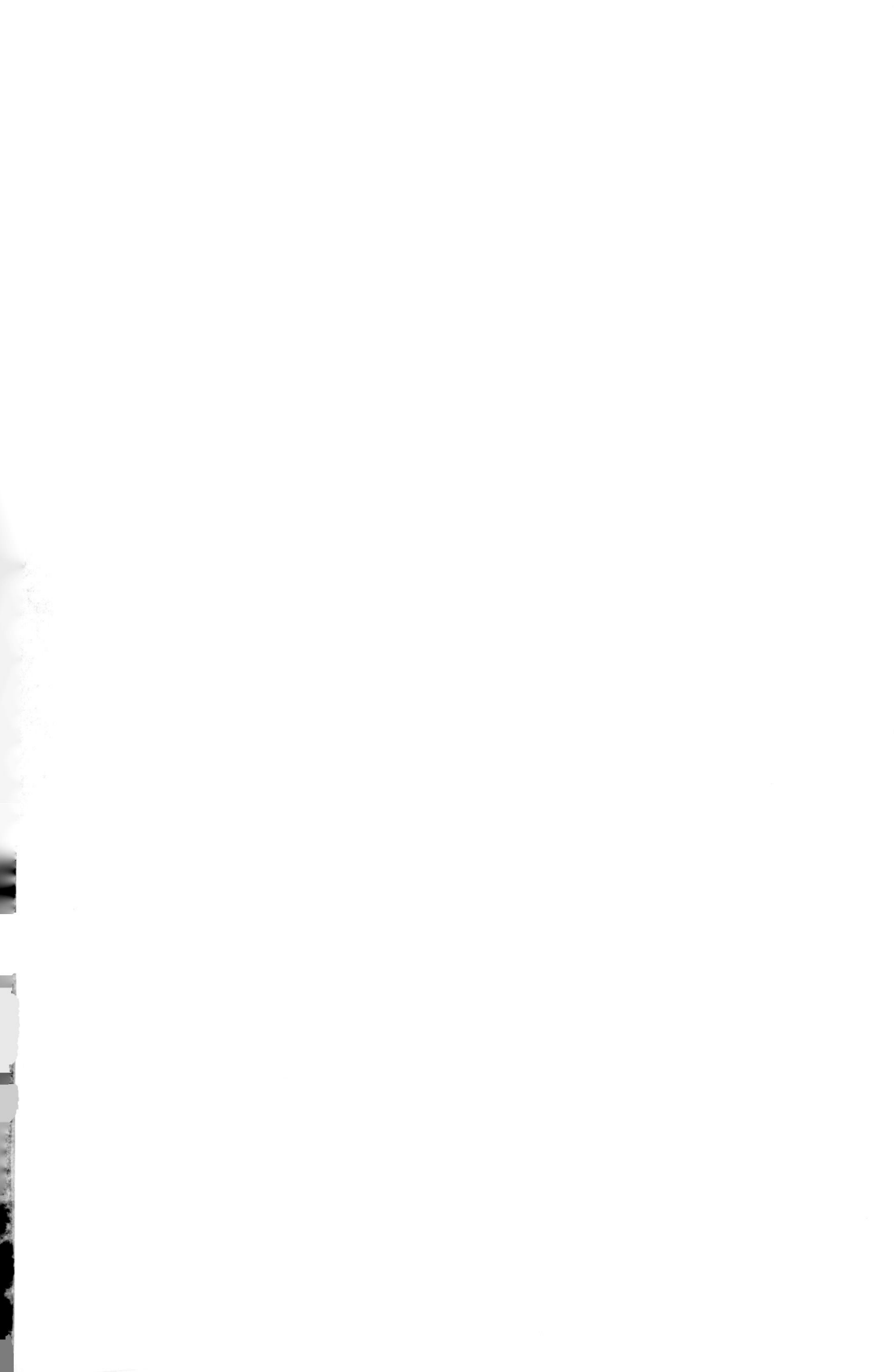

www.ingramcontent.com/pod-product-compliance
Lightning Source LLC
Chambersburg PA
CBHW040348220526
45473CB00009B/2813